THE DO'S

CHILD ACCESS AND VISITATION:

In the BEST INTEREST of the CHILD

A PLAN TO EFFECTIVE CO PARENTING

Prepared by: Rita U. McCain, BS, MA Conflict Resolution
Listed R31 Family*/General/Civil Mediator

Edited by: Nadine McNeal, DBH

Authors Copyright 000356
Published: Kindle Digital Publishing. July, 2022

Program made possible by:
Administrative Offices of the Court;
Parent Education Mediation Fund (TSC R38)

Presented by:
MAC'S MEDIATION
HENDERSON, TN 38340

*Special designation in Domestic Violence

This is where you are....

"Two people have a child together.

Maybe they were married?

Maybe dating?

Or maybe they were "just having sex"?

In this case, the "how" may not be as important as the "what" they produced – a beautiful soul who they have the opportunity to love and raise in this complicated world. It is real that working with another human to raise a little human is hard work. Parenting with a person that you otherwise would possibly have no contact with if given a choice is likely the hardest work that two people can do. Yes, many people do some version of this parenting life – often referenced as "co-parenting," (Grange, C. M.,Ph.D., et… 2021)

Having a problem with the other parent has nothing to do with the child. Had you taken more time to get to know this person, circumstances would be different. But here you are- sharing a lifetime commitment with somebody you know nothing about. As times goes on, you discover you don't even like this person- well too bad! That does not make them a bad person; just not the right person for you. BUT, they are the same person, for whatever reason, at the time, you chose to PROCREATE with. Unless you can prove this person is a bad influence on your child, and consistently has them in harm's way, you basically have to accept it. No two households are run the same, but where kids are concerned, they need to be close.

They deserve the best of both parents.

Deeper Look-[20 minutes discussion; list answers from participants on a board]
1. **What are two of your characteristics or habits would like to pass to your child?**
2. **What are two characteristics you have that you would not like for your child to mimic?**

The Exchange-

In a perfect world, both parents are in agreement with the co-parenting plan, kids are excited, and both parents adhere to the pick-up and drop off schedule. However, we do not live in a perfect world; nor are we perfect people. But here you are. Depending on the age of the child, you will be in this parenting agreement until this child turns 18, unless they change the law on age of consent.

When it comes time for the child to go to the other parent, this must be planned in advance and needs to be the same (or close as possible) for every visit (except in unforeseen circumstances). It's not "well we will be here" or I'll drop them off….. NO ! You need to be consistent! You know this visit is scheduled, so put your stuff on hold long enough for it to be a smooth transition, every time! This is a co-parenting relationship; nobody can make you enter into this agreement. The law can make you be financially responsible for your child; it takes more than money to be a Parent.

Communication is key, and with all the modern technology, there is no reason not to have consistent visitation with your child. There is video call with a cell phone. There is Yahoo Messenger, by phone, tablet or laptop. The messenger App will allow face to face communication, and allows the child to show, say a school project, or report card. This should be a private time between parent and child unless the visit is ordered to be supervised. Video calling via Zoom is also a safe way to conduct Mediation sessions on specific issues, without meeting in person. Zoom also allows for private or couple discussion at the control of the Mediator with the "waiting room".

Go to https://www.parents.com/parenting/best-co-parenting-apps/ for a list of Co Parenting Apps, which include shared calendars, scheduled, and other features to make the process easier.

Any communication with child, Co Parent or Mediator is best in person when possible.

Deeper Look- 20 min open discussion-
Let's discuss some options you would like to implement to provide consistent communication with the child and co-parent?

_____

_____

10 minute break

I'm waiting…….

If the other parent is not showing up as arranged or scheduled, can cause major issues for the other parent. It is rude, and shows a disrespect for the others persons time. It is also cruel to constantly lie to a child. If you know this is something you have scheduled until this child turns 18, or you change the plan, then everything else needs to be scheduled around that time. Now of course life happens; but there cannot be an excuse every scheduled or every other scheduled visitation. Treat the other persons time the same way you expect them to respect yours. This also sets up distrust of the missing parent and other people as the child gets older. It is not fair to the child to be consistently let down by the inconsistent parent. When this parent decides to show, the child's attitude can change. Just because you do decide to show, does not mean that the child has forget all the sadness from the previous "No Shows".

Most non-custodial parents use their visitation rights, as they agree, however some want visitation only when it's convenient; holding the custodial parent hostage waiting to see what the other parent will do. As we know, things come up, but "your emergency is not your child's emergency"; and again, the other parents has other plans. Another option before taking them back to Mediation, is to give a time limit. Get it understood, if they are more than 30 minutes late, the visit is cancelled. If their visitation is being cancelled due to their irresponsibility and they want to take you back to Mediation or Court, make sure to have notation of each incident. This may cause the inconsistent parent to get it together! The Court or Mediator will not look kindly on you wasting their time because of your own bad actions.

This type of inconsistency interferes with the psychological and emotional development of the child. These formed feelings carry on to adulthood and cause strain in most relationship because of these preconceived notions.

"Often a difficult process, co-parenting is greatly influenced by the reciprocal interactions of each parent. So, if you're parenting in a healthy way but your Ex isn't, your children will be at risk for developmental problems", (Serani, 2012).

Do not allow anybody to disappoint your child on a regular basis!

20 minute Break

Activity (2 hrs or less depending on size of group):

In groups (according to the age of children/child) of at least 3-6 participants; 1.Coustodial parent; 2. Child/children; 3 Co-parent; neutral party (grandparent, auntie, close family relative or friend). 15 min to prepare first skit.

a. Create a skit, in which the parent is a constant "no show". Demonstrate the effects it can have on the child at different ages. Think about the other parent; how this can cause a problem in their life. Also include how others can have an impact on the child/children.

b. each group will perform 1 skit, based on the child in different stages of life up to age 13. If child is 13, age 13 to 18. Include how the parent can also change over the years. Does the visits go good the first few years then start to change or vice versa?

c. These skits can be a part of your real life now, or as a child.

10 min break

This is happening…….

You have had a visitation schedule in place, and with the exception of a few variations over the past 3 years all has been going well. Then all of a sudden, the child does not want to go with the other parent. Why? What has changed? There was no complaints after the last visit, so where is this coming from? When you ask your child why they do not want to go because-

Reasons for not cancelling the visit-

1. I have a stomach ache or head ache- to appease the child, you check them over; you find no fever or other sign of illness.
2. I don't like the food.
3. I can't take my stuff.
4. They make me go to bed before I'm ready, and there is no TV in there.
5. We never do stuff together, they are on the computer or phone, and I get bored!

None of these are reasons to cancel the visit. If the child has a problem with the non-custodial parent, you encourage them to tell these things to the other parent, the same way they expressed them to you. Both parents must respect the rules of the other parents home.

Reasons that are caused for concern-

1. If you can prove this other person is involved in illegal, immoral, or abusive behavior.
2. Your child returns home from a visit, totally out of character. With a different demeanor, attitude, or behavior that was not there before.
3. If the child tell you the problem, and you know you and the other parent cannot have a conversation without it becoming a battle, then you need a neutral party that can help you have the conversation and not a screaming match!

If your child tells you something abusive has occurred, and you can see proof (physically or emotionally), then you will need to contact the proper authorities ASAP; do not wait until the next visit! Do not accuse a person of anything you cannot prove. If you feel this visit puts your child in danger, again, contact the proper authorities.

Children must know, in an age appropriate manner that "mommy and daddy could not get along, so the Court had to help us out, and if you don't go, we can get in trouble with the Courts. So since I know you will be safe, and cared for go get your stuff ready, because you are going". It is imperative that you [parents] present a united front, and do not hash it out in front of the child.

Do Not allow your child to manipulate the visitation. This teaches them they cannot do what they want, because they are a minor/under legal age, and it is your responsibility to do what is in their best interest. Again, keep the conversation age appropriate. Will they like it? Probably not. <u>But this is their new reality</u>. They follow your lead, so if you are helping in the adjustment, they are more likely to adapt. As parents, the biggest part of this position, is making decisions that will be in the best interest of your minor child/children.

Deeper Look- [Couple Activity 20 min]:

1. What will you consider a real reason to bring the other parent back to mediation?

Puberty changes things; visitation for teenagers ……..

At this age of your child's life, in their mind, they have a lot going on- Short word- Puberty. This stage in a child's development, is on steroids and your baby is now growing up. At this age, it may be time to rethink the parenting plan if it was started more than 5 yrs. ago. A teenager does not have the same needs as a younger child. This is the time to consider what's in the best interest of the child. Social development is taking place, the rules in regards to-

Education, extracurricular activities, friends, dating, chores, curfew, work, or any activity that involves the safety and welfare of the child, are issues for both parents. This is the time you need to be "on the same page or at least in the same book". Meaning, these rules are not expected to be exact in both households, however, children should not "run things" in one house that they do not run in the other home. Your methods may vary, but the goal should be the same- To raise a responsible, respectful, intelligent child that will mature into an upstanding productive, independent adult.

"Don't Make Unilateral Decisions or Changes to Status Quo"
"When parents have joint **decision-making**, don't make decisions on your own – it is bad co-parenting, and will hurt you. (Even if you have

sole decision-making, you almost always still have to keep the other parent informed). While if a court may not find all of the following examples to be actual violations worthy of contempt of court, you still hurt your case by making these kinds of decisions unilaterally:

- **"Medical** – selecting or changing doctors, or consenting to non-emergency treatment, therapy, etc
- **Education** – selecting or changing schools, tutoring, etc
- **Day Care** – selecting, changing or ending
- **Activities** – good to discuss regardless, but critical if it overlaps the other's time or the
  activity is potentially risky
- **Major Appearance Changes** – radical haircuts (or a child's first haircut), piercing or tattoos
- **Major Lifestyle Changes** – if a child never had vaccines, don't start unilaterally. If a child was raised vegetarian, don't start with meat unilaterally. It's not to say you are never allowed to do it, but talk to your attorney first.
- **Driver's License**

Sometimes it's a fine line between a major decision and a "day to day" decision which occurs wholly during your own time – if in doubt, you won't get accused of bad co-parenting for erring on the side of conferring. The opposite is not true, (Graham (?)). This is just one of the issues according to Graham in the Article entitled, "Bad Co-Parenting: 10 Ways to Kill Your Child Custody Case", (Graham (?)).

Again, children are not in charge of the visitation until they become of legal age. Leading up to this independence (between 13-18), more flexibility may be needed around the child's schedule. If by this time, you as parents, still have communication issues, it may become necessary to go back to Mediation. Just like you should not allow a child to stay home from school just because they don't want to go; that same applies to the visitation. It will not look very highly on your maturity or parenting skills if you have still have not learned how to get along.

This is not a time for the custodial parent or child to decide to cut back on the visitation. Besides the needs of the children changing, there should be a life changing (marriage;

death...) reason for the visitation to change. It needs to be a mutual decision, by the parents, at all time- keeping the best interest of the child as the deciding factor. Children will not always like the changes that you as the parent decide to make. This can be hard. My son did not want to move from IN to TN around age 10. I knew as a parent that if I raised my twins where we were, I would be in stiff competition with the gangs, drugs, and negative peer pressure. We agree today, it was not a bad move.

The law can force you to financially support your children, however, they cannot force you to be a Parent. So what type of parent are you?

Deeper Look 20-30 min.
In groups according to the age of the children, compose a list of 5 rules for children under 5; 5 rules for children 6-12; and five rules for children 13-18. House rules, school, going to Walmart.........

I don't have to do that over there…..

No two people parent the same way. Parenting is one of those jobs you don't know what your style will be until you are put in that situation. This does not make one person wrong or the other parent right-just different. However, their needs to be a meeting of the minds in some very important issues- let's discuss a few-

Safety- there needs to be a discussion or mutual agreement on how children are cared for and by whom. Now, you may not like the significant other of the other parent, however that is not a reason to cancel, change, or cut back on the visitation. Again, until your child reaches the age of legal consent, or an amendment is made, you are bound by the Parenting Plan on file with the Court.

Education- Hopefully both parents will be on the same page in this area. It is always in the best interest of the child to be encouraged to be the best they can be in all areas of life; UNTIL, they are able to make these decisions for themselves. After that point you have to find a way to communicate with your Adult Children; which is a whole other subject. You should always offer positive encouragement no matter the age.

If one parent is a stickler for homework, and good grades; how is that not in the best interest of the child? One parent feels your child should not be able to date before a certain age, and has a reasonable argument to support this decision it should be supported. There must be a united front, even if you agree to disagree. The same would be true if the other parent accept no excuse besides illness as a good reason to miss sports practice. Even though you feel it's too much, again, you may have to agree to disagree. Life is about compromise; no two people will always agree on every issue concerning the rearing of a child. Be reasonable. Even if you think you know the person before you had this child, still does not guarantee the perfect child, or best choice for a parent, but it will give you some idea of what to expect.

Chores- These need to be set up in some similarity in both homes. If the custodial parent has taught the child, at age 5, how to pick up his toys before going to bed; this behavior or as close as possible needs to become a practice in both homes. There should never be rules in one home that are not in the other, as close as possible. Do not ever tell the other parent you will do something, just to appease or shut them up, with no intention of doing it- it will eventually backfire, not to mention, send the wrong message to the child. Do not allow a child who has to follow the rules and has structure in one home, be allowed to total abandonment in the other home; again, it will backfire! In other words, you will grow to regret it, and change just may be too late.

Work-This needs to be a mutual decision, because if the child is being allowed to work arrangements have been made with inclusion of the visitation. Unless the child is of driving age, or has access to public transportation- both parents will need to have arrangements made for this to work out.

Also according to Dr. Serani, (2012), "Rules should be consistent and agreed upon at both households. As much as they fight it, children need routine and structure. Issues like meal time, bed time, and completing chores need to consistent. The same goes for school work and projects. Running a tight ship creates a sense of security and predictability for children".

Deeper Look [30 min.] Let's take a look at the rules from the last section. Put them in order of importance. Answers listed on board; then discussion on why and how to prioritize.

_____

_____

_____

_____

_____

Joint Activities

There will be activities that both parents will need to attend. Hopefully you have come to a point in the co-parenting relationship where you can be civil with each other. However, if your relationship has not progress to that point, be honest, and do not embarrass your child. Occasions when the child's entire family will be in attendance, and you have a good relationship with this side of the family, the child benefits most by seeing everyone being together and getting alone. According to Jennifer Wolf, (2020), "Having no problem attending school meetings, sporting events, and recitals when the other parent is present is another sign of an effective co-parenting relationship. She goes on to state, "These parents choose to put their children first and worries about what "others" think last, and are able to practice putting their own feelings about one another aside".

But if you know in advance there are family members you cannot be in the same space with, then stay away from each other. This has nothing to do with what you want- this is to keep the child from remembering this occasion in a negative way. Do you really want to be the cause of your child's (especially young children) shame because you don't like the maternal Aunt?

Holidays are noted in the Parenting Plan, as well as breaks from school. Be flexible. If you know it is important to the child, and it will not cause your world to fall apart, work it out. Remember, sometime before this whole parenting thing is done, you may need to same courtesy.

As children are expected to "act their age", so should parents. Children follow your lead, so if you show disdain for the other parent's family, children will do the same thing. Children need positive role models, and good examples to have a better chance of making better choices as they develop in all ways. If you have multiple children, then you have multiple issues. Of course, you love all your children, and want the best for them all. Then teach them from the choices you made; good and bad!

Moving forward

Your child does not have to know "all your Friends". It is best to not introduce young children to friends until you, the parent has known the person for at least a year. This may sound extreme, however, how well do you know the person you are bringing around your child?? And just because you seem to have a connection with this person, what happens in 6 months, when it does not work? Below are 5 things to consider before introducing your children to your new partner-

Here are the 5 Rules for Introducing Your New Partner to Your Kids

1. Timing is essential to healthy family adjustment after divorce.

2. Keep in mind that your kids may view your new love as a rival.

3. Consider your children's needs for security and reassurance

4. Ask yourself: Is my love interest a good fit for my family?

5. Invite your children's feedback for ideas about how and when they meet your new   partner for the first time, (Gaspard, 2021).

Do not bring home a "friend" when your child is there. This is time for you to be the other part of this co- parenting team. You will not get these years in your child's life back; no do overs. Your time with your child has to be about them- not you and whatever you may have going on when the child is with the other parent. This is not to say, don't pursue other relationships; just not on your child's time; until your know as much as possible about this new person do not have them around your child. Remember, your child already has two parents-the two people that enter into this agreement.

Now if you happen to be living with your significant other, they are not your "baby sitter", or the child's parent; your schedule should still be around your child's visitation. If there is a conversation, between you and your child, this other person needs to stay out of it! They can share their concerns in private. Think about it-Would you want the significant other of the other parent to interfere? Children do not need to be included in adult conversations.

In the best interest of the child, be very careful; they do what you do- not always what you say. Keep them safe, set good examples, and prepare them for the world. They will not be child a always; but they will always be your child.

Deeper Look- 30 min discussion-
1. How do you see this working out?
2. What will you do extra if needed, to make this work?
3. What will you not do?

_____

_____

_____

_____

_____

_____

_____

THINGS YOU DO NOT WANT TO FORGET TO DISCUSS IN PRIVATE MEDIATION

By the way………

I was a single parent to a set of twins, born 3 weeks before my 26th birthday. Parenting is one of the hardest, most rewarding experiences in life. Children are not born with a manual. We all do the best we can with what we know. However age, maturity level, education, social, and economic background all contribute to our idea of parenthood. Good, bad or indifferent-it is what it is; but it does not have to be.

I tell my own children, keep the good I taught you and pass it on to your own children. But if there was something you can do different or better to achieve a better outcome, then do what you think is best for your children. Our children grow up. During this time they need boundaries, expectation, constant encouragement and praise. They also have to learn consequences and accountability. And as they grow older, things instilled in them during this time of life plays a major whole in their success as an adult and parent. There are no "do overs" in life, and you cannot raise adults. No matter how hard you try to do what is in their best interest as children, there is no guarantee's in this life. When my own adult children say or do things I don't agree with, I take solace in knowing I did the best I could with what I knew how and what I learned along the way. My last child was born when I was 36, and I was married to her father for almost 10 years, until she was about 7, then it was back to being a single parent. We all have choices to make, and we have to live with those choices. But we must learn from those choices as well.

Rita

RIGHTS OF PARENTS

Under T.C.A. § 36-6-101 of Tennessee law, both parents are entitled to the following rights:

(1) The right to unimpeded telephone conversations with the child at least twice a week at reasonable times and for reasonable durations. The parent exercising parenting time shall furnish the other parent with a telephone number where the child may be reached at the days and time specified in a parenting plan or other court order or, where days and times are not specified, at reasonable times;

(2) The right to send mail to the child which the other parent shall not destroy, deface, open or censor. The parent exercising parenting time shall deliver all letters, packages and other material sent to the child by the other parent as soon as received and shall not interfere with their delivery in any way, unless otherwise provided by law or court order;

(3) The right to receive notice and relevant information as soon as practicable but within twenty-four (24) hours of any hospitalization, major illness or injury, or death of the child. The parent exercising parenting time when such event occurs shall notify the other parent of the event and shall provide all relevant healthcare providers with the contact information for the other parent;

(4) The right to receive directly from the child's school any educational records customarily made available to parents. Upon request from one parent, the parent enrolling the child in school shall provide to the other parent as soon as available each academic year the name, address, telephone number and other contact information for the school. In the case of children who are being homeschooled, the parent providing the homeschooling shall advise the other parent of this fact along with the contact information of any sponsoring entity or other entity involved in the child's education, including access to any individual student records or grades available online. The school or homeschooling entity shall be responsible, upon request, to provide to each parent records customarily made available to parents. The school may require a written request which includes a current mailing address and may further require payment of the reasonable costs of duplicating such records. These records include copies of the child's report cards, attendance records, names of teachers, class schedules, and standardized test scores;

(5) Unless otherwise provided by law, the right to receive copies of the child's medical, health or other treatment records directly from the treating physician or healthcare provider. Upon request from one parent, the parent who has arranged for such treatment or health care shall provide to the other parent the name, address, telephone number and other contact information of the physician or healthcare provider. The keeper of the records may require a written request including a current mailing address and may further require payment of the reasonable costs of duplicating such records. No person who receives the mailing address of a requesting parent as a result of this requirement shall provide such address to the other parent or a third person;

(6) The right to be free of unwarranted derogatory remarks made about such parent or such parent's family by the other parent to or in the

presence of the child;
(7) The right to be given at least forty-eight (48) hours notice, whenever possible, of all extracurricular school, athletic, church activities and other activities as to which parental participation or observation would be appropriate, and the opportunity to participate in or observe them. The parent who has enrolled the child in each such activity shall advise the other parent of the activity and provide contact information for the person responsible for its scheduling so that the other parent may make arrangements to participate or observe whenever possible, unless otherwise provided by law or court order;
(8) The right to receive from the other parent, in the event the other parent leaves the state with the minor child or children for more than forty-eight (48) hours, an itinerary which shall include the planned dates of departure and return, the intended destinations and mode of travel and telephone numbers. The parent traveling with the child or children shall provide this information to the other parent so as to give that parent reasonable notice; and
(9) The right to access and participation in the child's education on the same bases that are provided to all parents including the right of access to the child during lunch and other school activities; provided, that the participation or access is legal and reasonable; however, access must not interfere with the school's day-to-day operations or with the child's educational schedule.

VII. NOTICE REGARDING PARENTAL RELOCATION

The Tennessee statute (T.C.A. § 36-6-108) which governs the notice to be given in connection with the relocation of a parent reads in pertinent part as follows:
If a parent who is spending intervals of time with a child desires to relocate outside the state or more than fifty (50) miles from the other parent within the state, the relocating parent shall send a notice to the other parent at the other parent's last known address by registered or certified mail. Unless excused by the court for exigent circumstances, the notice shall be mailed not later than sixty (60) days prior to the move. The notice shall contain the following:
(1) Statement of intent to move;
(2) Location of proposed new residence;
(3) Reasons for proposed relocation; and
(4) Statement that the other parent may file a petition in opposition to the move within thirty (30) days of receipt of the notice.

VIII. PARENT EDUCATION CLASS

This requirement has been fulfilled by ☐ both parents ☐ mother ☐ father ☐ neither.
Failure to attend the parent education class within 60 days of this order is punishable by contempt.

Works Cited

Gaspard, T., (2021). *5 Rules for Introducing a New Partner to Your Kids After Divorce.* Retrieved from https://www.divorcemag.com/blog/5-rules-for-introducing-new-partner-to-kids on July 5, 2022

Graham, C.O., (?). *Bad Co-Parenting: 10 Ways to Kill Your Child Custody Case.* Retrieved from https://www.colorado-family-law.com/parenting-custody/bad-co-parenting-kill-child-custody-case on July 8, 2022.

Grange, C. M., Ph.D., Harris, C., Ph.D. and Williams, A. Ph.D. (2021), For the Souls of Black Folks. *What Is Co-Parenting? Understanding complexities to help move towards possible realities.* Retrieved from https://www.psychologytoday.com/us/blog/the-souls-black-folks/202106/what-is-co-parenting on July 8, 2022.

Serani, D., Psy D. (2012). The Do's and Don'ts of Co-Parenting Well *Effective problem solving tips and approaches.* Psychology Today. Retrieved from https://www.psychologytoday.com/us/blog/two-takes-depression/201203/the-dos-and-donts-co-parenting-well on July 8, 2022.

Wolf, J., (2020). *10 Signs of a Healthy, Effective Co-Parenting Relationship.* Retrieved from https://www.verywellfamily.com/signs-of-a-healthy-coparenting-relationship-2997282 on July 8, 2022.

NOTES

Made in the USA
Columbia, SC
23 August 2022

YOUNG HERO TRAINING MANUAL

21 DAILY DEVOTIONS FOR CHILDREN

DR. AARON GEORGE GLOVER

www.theboomsquad.com

The Boom Squad: Young Hero Training Manual
21 Daily Devotionals For Children
Text copyright © 2025 by Aaron George Glover, Ed.D.
Illustrations copyright © 2025 by Aaron George Glover, Ed.D.
Published by Aaron George Glover, Ed.D.
For more information, visit www.theboomsquad.com

All rights reserved. No part of this publication may be reproduced, stored in a retrieval system, or transmitted in any form or by any means - electronic, mechanical, photocopy, recording, printing, or any other - except for brief quotations in printed reviews, without prior permission of the publisher.

Hey there Boom Squad Buddies! It's Bebot here, ready to show you how to use this daily devotional to help you become the hero God created you to be! Each day has a theme that is explored in 3 parts: Power, Ponder, and Pray!

- **POWER** - This is where we dive into a Bible truth that teaches us about being faithful heroes.
- **PONDER** - This is the part where we think about what the Bible truth means and how it can help us in our daily lives.
- **PRAY** - We finish with a short prayer, thanking God and asking Him to help us live heroic lives.

Are you ready to get started? Let's go, heroes!

MEET THE SQUAD!

BABOOM

The bold boomerang-wielding leader of the Boom Squad! When danger strikes, he's the first to stand tall and lead the charge against the bad guys. His dream is to become a great hero like his dad, the Mighty Blast Captain! Baboom is a team captain, a trustworthy friend, and a true faith-filled hero!

BUSTER

The fearless Boomstick-swinging Vanguard of the Boom Squad! Always ready for action, Buster charges into battle with courage and a contagious smile. Whether he's leaping into the fray or training for the next adventure, Buster brings explosive energy and unstoppable faith to everything he does!

BEBOT & BLAST CAPTAIN

The Clever Sidekick of the Boom Squad! With quick thinking and a heart of gold, Bebot supports his team with gadgets, wisdom, and unwavering loyalty. While he never steps into battle, Bebot plays a crucial role from the Treehouse Headquarters, providing critical intel and guidance to the squad!

The legendary hero, fearless father, and the inspiration behind the Boom Squad. He's the greatest hero on Earth! Even when battle-worn, he rises with strength rooted in God, showing us that true power comes from above. He's training the Boom Squad to become the next generation of great heroes!

YOUNG HERO TRAINING LESSONS

Day   Topic

1. The Power of Faith in Jesus
2. A Hero is Strong in the Lord
3. Being a Brave Hero
4. Lifting Others Up
5. A Hero is Always Honest
6. The Power of Patience
7. A Hero is Always Learning
8. Handmade by God
9. A Hero Judges Fairly
10. The Power of Forgiveness
11. The Greatness of Serving
12. Filled with True Joy
13. Be a Loyal Friend
14. The Power of Hope
15. A Hardworking Hero
16. Shine Your Light!
17. The Power of Prayer
18. A Hero is Level-Headed
19. The Power of Obedience
20. Using Your Gifts
21. A New Creation in Christ

DAY 1

THE POWER OF FAITH IN JESUS

"For God so loved the world, that He gave His only Son, that whoever believes in Him should not perish but have eternal life." (John 3:16)

POWER

Jesus Christ is the greatest hero in the Bible! He is the only person to ever live a perfect life, to fully please God, and to save humanity from their sins. All He asks is that we put our faith and trust in Him as Lord and Savior. When we believe in Jesus, He changes us into a new person- we become heroes like Him! Faith in Jesus is the key to living the heroic life that God has for you (2 Corinthians 5:16-21).

PONDER

Jesus left heaven and came to Earth so that He could rescue us from our sin. He was truly heroic in every way! He loved God and loved people — and He wants us to do that too. When you believe in Jesus, He saves you and makes you a hero. How can you live heroically like Jesus? How can you love God and love others?

PRAY

Dear God, You are the true hero! Thank you for saving me from my sin and making me like Your Son, Jesus. Help me be a hero like Jesus. Grow my faith, my love for You, and my love for others. Amen!

DAY 2

A HERO IS STRONG IN THE LORD

"Be strong in the Lord and in His mighty power."
(Ephesians 6:10)

POWER

Super strength is a power that many superheroes have. You may think strength is just about big muscles, but the Bible teaches us that we have a strength far greater than that... We have the strength of the Lord! The same power that defeated sin and death is now alive in us so that we can be strong like Jesus. God has given us His strength to serve Him and help others!

PONDER

True strength is more than just muscles. You can be strong in your heart, in your mind, and in your faith!
Think of ways that you want to be strong in the Lord. Maybe you want to be stronger in your faith, your patience, or your self-control... How can you practice using God's strength in different ways like these?

PRAY

Dear God, You are the source of my strength! Help me to be strong in my heart, mind, body, and faith! Teach me to use my strength to serve You and to help others. Amen!

DAY 3

BEING A BRAVE HERO

"Have I not commanded you? Be strong and courageous. Do not be frightened, and do not be dismayed, for the Lord your God is with you wherever you go." (Joshua 1:9)

POWER

Every hero feels afraid sometimes. They may be afraid of trying something new, facing a big challenge, or doing a scary thing. In the Bible, Joshua had a tough job as he led Israel into the Promised Land, but God said He would be with Joshua every step of the way (Joshua 1:1-9). Instead of living in fear, Joshua lived in faith. He was a brave leader, and God used him to lead the people of Israel to victory!

PONDER

How do you think Joshua felt when he was leading Israel's army into battle? He may have been afraid. How do you think he felt when he remembered God's promise to be with him? He may have still been afraid, but he trusted God and kept going! How can you be brave like Joshua?

PRAY

Dear God, Help me to be brave when I feel afraid. Help me to forget my fears and to remember Your promises! I want to be a brave hero like Joshua- he was a faithful man who trusted You and led people to victory. You make me brave. Amen!

DAY 4

LIFTING OTHERS UP

"Therefore encourage one another and build one another up, just as you are doing."
(1 Thessalonians 5:11)

POWER

A hero uses their strength to lift others up! In the Bible, the Apostle Paul wrote many letters to Christians to help build up their faith and strengthen their relationships with others. He said things like "carry each other's burdens" and "help the weak." The Bible says that we have all been given gifts to help build up and serve the church. It is important for us to use our gifts for the good of others—to lift them up!

PONDER

How does it feel when you read an encouraging card? A thank you note? Or a letter of congratulations? It feels great! That is exactly how Paul lifted others up in the Bible- He wrote letters! Is there someone you could write a nice card to? What is another way you could lift up someone or encourage them?

PRAY

Dear God, Thank You for all the times You have made me feel good. Thank you for all the people in my life who encourage me and lift me up! Help me encourage others, show me ways I can remind them of how wonderful and loved they are. Amen!

DAY 5

A HERO IS ALWAYS HONEST

"An honest witness tells the truth, but a false witness tells lies."
(Proverbs 12:17)

POWER

Sometimes, a hero may be tempted to lie. But we should remember that the Bible says that lies are from the devil; they are something that he uses to trick, deceive, and trap people. A hero should never tell lies because a hero was made to walk in the truth, just like Jesus. Every time Jesus was asked a question, He gave an honest answer. He never lied, and we shouldn't either.

PONDER

Have you ever felt bad after telling a lie? Sometimes, one small lie leads to another and another until it makes a big mess of lies, trouble, and pain.

On the other hand, have you ever felt good after telling the truth, even when it was hard? How can you practice honesty the next time you are tempted to lie?

PRAY

Dear God, I know that You are the God of truth! You never lie and neither should I! Help me to walk in the truth whenever I am tempted to lie. Remind me that lies are like a prison, but the truth sets me free! Amen!

DAY 6

THE POWER OF PATIENCE

"God told Abraham, "Look up and number the stars... So shall your offspring be." And Abraham believed the Lord, and God counted it to him as righteousness."
(Genesis 15:5-6)

POWER

Abraham is a great hero of faith who waited patiently for God's promises. When Abraham was 75, God told him he would have a son (Genesis 12:1-4). After 25 years of waiting, when Abraham was 100, his son Isaac was finally born (Genesis 21:5)!

The Bible calls Abraham the father of faith because he trusted God, even when it seemed impossible (Romans 4:20-21). Like Abraham, we should trust God and wait for His perfect timing!

PONDER

Have you ever felt impatient? Maybe you wanted to cut in line for something at school, or maybe you were excited for an upcoming event. So, how can you be patient like Abraham?

The next time you feel impatient, try to slow down and remember that God has perfect timing in your life.

PRAY

Dear God, Please help me practice patience. Show me how to be patient with myself and with other people. You are patient with me; I want to be patient like You. Teach me to wait faithfully like Abraham. Amen!

DAY 7

A HERO IS ALWAYS LEARNING

"Give me wisdom and knowledge, that I may lead these people, for who is able to govern this great people of yours?"
(2 Chronicles 1:10)

POWER

The great King Solomon knew that good leadership required wisdom and knowledge- so that's what he asked God to give him! He could have asked God for anything in the world... but he chose to ask for something that would help him be a good person and a good leader (1 Kings 3:5-12). We can be wise like Solomon if we continue to learn and grow every single day!

PONDER

What would you do if you were the smartest person on the planet? How would you use all that knowledge?
Maybe you would invent new technology or solve a big problem... Now think, what would God want you to do?

PRAY

Dear God, I want to learn and grow every day! I want to be wise in my thoughts and actions. Please help me to be a hero that is always learning and growing. I want to learn all I can about You and Your creation. Amen!

Hey there, Hero!
Congratulations on finishing the first 7 days of your heroic journey. Each one of these devotionals helps you grow into the hero that God created you to be! I know that you have what it takes to make an incredible impact on the world.

Always remember that God made you for great things!

DAY 8
HANDMADE BY GOD

"For You created my inmost being; You knit me together in my mother's womb. I praise You because I am fearfully and wonderfully made..."
(Psalm 139:13-14)

POWER

Every hero was handmade by God, including YOU! The Bible says God purposefully and specifically made you. He designed you with love and care because He has a purpose for your life. The Bible also says God made us in His image, meaning we should reflect Him to the world (Genesis 1:26-27). Remember, God wants you to become a great hero of faith, and make a heroic difference in the world for His kingdom!

PONDER

Did you know that you were handmade by God?
Paul tells Christians that they are "God's masterpiece, created in Christ Jesus to do good works, which He prepared in advance for us to walk in" (Ephesians 2:10).
How does it make you feel to be called God's "masterpiece"?

PRAY

Dear God, Thank you for creating me! I know that You made me with purpose and have a special mission for my life. I want to become a great hero of faith, just like You want me to be. You prepared good works for me to walk in, and I am proud to be your masterpiece in Christ. Amen!

DAY 9
A HERO JUDGES FAIRLY

"Do not pervert justice; do not show partiality to the poor or favoritism to the great, but judge your neighbor fairly."
(Leviticus 19:15)

POWER

A hero always treats everyone fairly! When Nehemiah found out that some of the leaders were unfairly charging the poor Jews too much, he knew he had to do something. He called a meeting and told the leaders to stop being unfair and to give back everything they had wrongly taken. The leaders listened to Nehemiah and agreed to do what was right. Everyone worked together to make things fair again! (Nehemiah 5:1-13)

PONDER

Have you ever been treated unfairly? How did you feel? Remember, everyone deserves to be treated fairly.
How can you help make sure that everyone is treated the same? Think of some ways you can help everyone feel included and respected.

PRAY

Dear God, I want to be a fair hero! Help me to be kind and respectful to everyone, just like Nehemiah. Thank You for showing me how to stand up for others and treat everyone fairly. Amen!

DAY 10

THE POWER OF FORGIVENESS

"Be kind and compassionate to one another, forgiving each other, just as in Christ God forgave you."
(Ephesians 4:32)

POWER

Forgiveness is heroic! The greatest hero ever, Jesus, especially showed this incredible power while He was being crucified. Even as He was suffering on the cross, Jesus prayed for the people who were hurting Him. He said, "Father, forgive them, for they do not know what they are doing" (Luke 23:34). Jesus offers forgiveness to everybody, so we should too!

PONDER

If Jesus forgave us, we should forgive others.
Instead of staying angry with someone, you can choose to forgive them. Your forgiveness will bless them and YOU!
Can you think of someone who needs your forgiveness?

PRAY

Dear God, I want to be a forgiving hero just like Jesus! Whenever someone wrongs me, remind me of Your forgiveness. Thank you for forgiving me! Because I am forgiven, I want to forgive too. Amen!

DAY 11

THE GREATNESS OF SERVING

"The Son of Man did not come to be served, but to serve, and to give his life as a ransom for many."
(Matthew 20:28)

POWER

The greatest heroes are the greatest servants. When the disciples asked Jesus how to become great leaders, He taught them about the power of serving! Jesus told them that the way to become a great leader was through being a great servant. At the Last Supper, Jesus washed his disciples' feet as an example of how they should serve one another. He showed them true greatness through service! (John 13:3-17)

PONDER

Jesus is the King of the universe, yet He became a humble servant and gave His life to help others. Why did He do that? If Jesus used His power to serve others and take care of them, we should too! Who are some people you can serve?

PRAY

Dear God, I want to be a great servant like King Jesus! He used His power to help others in need. Show me ways that I can help serve others in the same way. Thank You for showing me the power of serving. Amen!

DAY 12
FILLED WITH TRUE JOY

"Rejoice in the Lord always; again I will say, rejoice."
(Philippians 4:4)

POWER

Faithful heroes are filled with joy! The Apostle Paul knew the importance of rejoicing in the Lord, even when bad things were happening. One time, Paul and Silas were put into prison for preaching about Jesus. But instead of being sad, they sang worship songs all night. Suddenly, an earthquake shook the prison and their chains fell off! They were free, and they used that miracle to tell their jailer about Jesus! (Acts 16:25-34)

PONDER

Paul faced many challenges while sharing the message of Jesus. Yet, he always rejoiced in God, even when bad things happened. Paul had a joy that nothing in the world could take away. So, where did Paul's joy come from? It came from God! How can we be joyful like Paul?

PRAY

Dear God, Thank you for giving me Your joy in Christ Jesus! I want to be joyful, just like Paul. No matter what happened to him, he always rejoiced in You. Help me rejoice in You always, no matter what happens. Amen!

DAY 13
BE A LOYAL FRIEND

"Never let loyalty and kindness leave you! Tie them around your neck as a reminder. Write them deep within your heart."
(Proverbs 3:3)

POWER

Heroes are loyal to God and their friends! Jonathan was the son of King Saul and was David's best friend. When King Saul became jealous of David and wanted to hurt him, Jonathan warned David of his father's evil plan. Jonathan knew God had chosen David to become king, so he helped David escape and protected him. Even though it was a very hard time, Jonathan was a loyal friend to David. (1 Samuel 18-23)

PONDER

Loyalty means that we love someone and do what is best for them at all times, especially during hard times. Do you have a best friend that you are loyal toward?
How can you show loyalty to your friends?
What are some ways you can show loyalty to God?

PRAY

Dear God, I want to be a loyal follower of You! I also want to be a loyal friend. Help me to love my friends like Jonathan did. He was there for his friend, David. Thank You for teaching me true loyalty. Amen!

DAY 14

THE POWER OF HOPE

"Do not be afraid. Stand firm and you will see the deliverance the Lord will bring you today."
(Exodus 14:13)

POWER

For over 400 years, the Jews were slaves in Egypt. The book of Exodus tells how God used a man named Moses to bring them a message of hope and freedom from slavery. After God sent 10 plagues upon Egypt, Pharaoh finally let the Jews go. But soon after, Pharaoh changed his mind and began chasing them. The Jews were trapped between the Egyptian army and the Red Sea. Their only hope was to trust in God! Miraculously, God parted the Red Sea, and the Jews crossed safely. When Pharaoh's army tried to follow, the waters crashed down on them! The Jews trusted God, and He saved them!

PONDER

God always keeps His promises! Throughout the Bible, we see God saving His people again and again. He never fails and He never will. This is why we put our hope in Him. Do you believe that God keeps His promises?

PRAY

Dear God, Thank You for always keeping Your promises! The Jews put their hope and trust in You, and You saved them. I know that You will keep all of Your promises to me too. I believe You and I trust Your love for me. Amen!

Hey there, Hero!
You are doing a great job of growing as a faithful hero in Christ. When God created you, he gave you specific gifts and talents that he wants you to use for the good of others. Practice using these gifts to help serve others and point them to Jesus!

Remember, God made you for great things!

DAY 15
A HARDWORKING HERO

"Whatever you do, work heartily, as for the Lord and not for men."
(Colossians 3:23)

POWER

Hard work pays off! When Nehemiah heard that the walls of Jerusalem were in ruins, he decided to rebuild them. He put together a plan and worked hard, even when people tried to discourage him and stop him. Nehemiah stayed focused on his work and eventually completed the project. The walls of Jerusalem were rebuilt! Nehemiah showed us that God's missions may require hard work and persistence. Plus, we can trust that God will complete whatever He starts!
(Read Nehemiah 1-6 for the full story of this great work!)

PONDER

Nehemiah stayed focused on his mission to rebuild the wall. How can you stay focused on your goals?
Nehemiah also inspired others with his faith and work ethic. How can you inspire or encourage others?

PRAY

Dear God, Thank You for Nehemiah's example of faithfulness and hard work. Help me to work hard and stay focused on the tasks in my life. I know that You will help me and strengthen me. Amen!

DAY 16

SHINE YOUR LIGHT!

"For you were once darkness, but now you are light in the Lord. Live as children of light."
(Ephesians 5:8)

POWER

Being in a dark room can feel really scary sometimes. What's the first thing you do? You turn on a light! Suddenly, the scary and unknown things in the darkness aren't so frightening because the light reveals the truth—there's nothing to be afraid of! The world can feel like a dark and scary place too. But God has given you something special—His light (His life)! He gave it to you so that you can shine His light into the darkness and help others see the truth about His love and goodness. So, let your light shine!

PONDER

How can you shine the light of Jesus into the world? In Matthew 5, Jesus taught us to let our light shine before others, so they may see our good deeds and praise God. What are 3 ways you can show God's light to others? Write them down and try them out this week!

PRAY

Dear God, Thank you for giving me Your light- Your life! I want to shine Your light everywhere I go, just like Jesus did. Show me how I can lead people out of darkness and into Your marvelous light. Amen!

DAY 17
THE POWER OF PRAYER

"The prayer of a righteous person is powerful and effective"
(James 5:16)

POWER

Prayer is one of the greatest powers you have! In 1 Samuel 1, a faithful woman named Hannah was very sad because she did not have any children. Instead of giving up hope, she faithfully prayed to God and asked for a son. Hannah made a promise to God: if He gave her a son, she would dedicate him to serve the Lord. God heard Hannah's prayer and answered her! She later gave birth to Samuel, who grew up to become a great prophet of God.

PONDER

Our prayers are powerful because God hears them and cares about us! We can bring anything and everything to God in prayer. What are some things you want to pray about? Remember, God loves to hear from you!

PRAY

Dear God, Thank You for hearing my prayers and caring about me. I know that You answer prayers, just like when You helped Hannah. I know that I can talk to You about anything when I pray. Thank You for loving me and listening to my prayers. Amen!

DAY 18

A HERO IS LEVEL-HEADED

"...Everyone should be quick to listen, slow to speak and slow to become anger, because human anger does not produce the righteousness that God desires."
(James 1:19-20)

POWER

Controlling our anger is one of the greatest super powers of faith! Look at Joseph in the book of Genesis: His brothers betrayed him into slavery which caused him great suffering. Many years later, they came to him for food because of a drought in their land. Instead of staying angry with them, Joseph chose to love and forgive them. He even invited all of their families to come live with him! (Genesis 45:3-15)

PONDER

What should we do when we get really mad or upset?
Here are 3 things you can do to help control your emotions:
1. Take a deep breath and count to ten
2. Say a quick prayer, asking God for help
3. Walk away for a moment to think

PRAY

Dear God, I want to be a level-headed hero! Help me whenever I get angry or lose my cool. Remind me that I can make good choices whenever I get upset. I want to be like Joseph. Help me choose love over anger. Amen!

DAY 19

THE POWER OF OBEDIENCE

"Noah did this; he did all that God commanded him."
(Genesis 6:22)

POWER

Obedience is more than just following the rules; it is about following God with your heart, mind, and actions! Noah is a great example of faithful obedience to the Lord. When God told Noah to build an ark because a flood was coming, Noah trusted God and obeyed (Genesis 6:13-22). Because of his obedience, Noah, his family, and numerous animals were saved from the flood! God knows what is best for us, so it is important for us to listen to Him and obey His commands.

PONDER

When God speaks, we should listen and obey. After all, He knows everything and wants good things for us. He wants us to live good lives that honor him and help others.
Why is it sometimes hard to obey God?
What can you do to be more obedient to Him?

PRAY

Dear God, I want to obey You, just like Noah! I know that You care about me and want me to live a good life that honors You and leads others to Jesus. Help me to obey You with my heart, mind, and actions. You know the way I should go, and I want to follow You. Amen!

DAY 20

USING YOUR GIFTS

"Each of you should use the gift you have received to serve others, as faithful stewards of God's grace in various forms."
(1 Peter 4:10)

POWER

The Bible says that every believer has been given spiritual gifts to serve one another! Maybe you have the gift of speaking, helping, or teaching. Whatever your gift is, God wants you to use it to help and build up others! The Bible teaches us that all of these gifts come from the Holy Spirit, and they are all important to the body of Christ—other Christians. We should use our gifts with love, to serve others and make them stronger in their faith.

PONDER

Talk to your teacher or another grown-up about the gifts they see in you. Sometimes, they can see things that you haven't noticed yet! Talk about why each of these gifts is important, and think of ways you can use them to help others!

PRAY

Dear God, Thank You for giving me spiritual gifts! I know that every gift is important and can be used to make a big difference in the world. I want to use my gifts to help others and point them to Jesus. Thank you for empowering me to be a hero for You. Amen!

DAY 21

A NEW CREATION IN CHRIST

"Therefore, if anyone is in Christ, they are a new creation: The old has gone, the new is here!"
(2 Corinthians 5:17)

POWER

Whenever we believe in Jesus, several things happen! The Bible says that He saves us and changes us from the inside out! We become a "new creation" with a new heart, a new spirit, and a new life! All of our sins and mistakes are forgiven and we become free to live as the heroes God created us to be. We become people who live by faith, following the guidance of the Holy Spirit. We have a new life in Christ!

PONDER

Have you ever had a toy that got worn out or broken after a long time? If you couldn't fix the damage, you likely threw it away or quit playing with it. But what if you could have made it brand new and better than before? That's what God did to you! Instead of casting you aside, He made you completely new and gave you eternal life!

PRAY

Dear God, Thank You for making me new in Christ Jesus. Thank You for forgiving my sins and giving me a new life! Help me to live each day as a new creation, walking by faith and led by the Holy Spirit. Amen!

Hey there, Hero!
Every day, you have a chance to make good choices and do heroic deeds. It is not always easy, but God will always help you and give you the strength you need. Plus, the Boom Squad is here to help you become a great hero who loves God and helps other people!

God made you for great things!

LEARN MORE AT THEBOOMSQUAD.COM

NOW AVAILABLE!

The Boom Squad: Attack of the Go-Bots

When an army of Vylex's Go-bots attacks the city park, Baboom and Buster must find a way to stop them. Be careful boys... The Go-bots are small but they are quick, strong, and under Vylex's control!

JOIN THE ADVENTURE!

JESUS SAVES US!

1. God Loves You!
God made the whole world and everything in it. The most special part of His creation is people— like you! God loves you more than you can imagine, and He wants to be your best friend forever! The Bible teaches that God loves us so much that He sent His Son, Jesus, so we could have eternal life and be with Him forever! (1 John 4:9-10).

2. Sin Separates Us from God
But there's a problem. Sometimes we do things that are wrong—like lying, being unkind, or disobeying. These wrong things are called "sin", and sin separates us from God because He is perfect and holy. The Bible says that we have all sinned and been separated from God (Romans 3:23).

3. Jesus Came to Save Us
Now, here's the Good News! Jesus loves you so much, that He willingly took the punishment for your sins. Jesus lived a perfect life, died on the cross in your place, and then rose from the dead. Because of Jesus, you can be forgiven and have a friendship with God forever! The Bible says, "For God so loved the world that He gave His one and only Son, that whoever believes in Him shall not perish but have eternal life" (John 3:16).

4. You Can Be Friends with God
To become friends with God, all you need to do is believe in Jesus and what He did for you. You can talk to God in a prayer and tell Him you're sorry for your sins, thank Him for sending Jesus, and ask Him to be your Savior and best friend forever. The Bible says, "If you confess with your mouth, 'Jesus is Lord,' and believe in your heart that God raised Him from the dead, you will be saved" (Romans 10:9).

5. You Become a New Creation
When you believe in Jesus, you become a new creation! You become God's best friend— You are forgiven, declared righteous, given the Holy Spirit, and made spiritually alive forever! Faith in Jesus saves us from the punishment of our sins and gives us new life in His name. Now you can live a new and heroic life with your Lord and Savior, Jesus Christ!

ABOUT THE CREATOR

Dr. Aaron George Glover is a passionate creator, author, and devoted follower of Christ. With a heart for inspiring others, he combines his love for God and creativity to craft stories that empower children with heroic lessons from Scripture. Dr. Glover earned his Doctorate in Educational Leadership with an emphasis on Educational Ministry Leadership from Dallas Baptist University (2020). His educational journey, ministry experience, and artistic talents have uniquely positioned him to weave biblical truths into a series of powerful and life-changing creative works: The Boom Squad.

When he's not writing or teaching, Dr. Glover enjoys spending time with his family, reading great books, playing guitar, working out, and exploring new avenues to fuel his creative passions!

To learn more, visit www.theboomsquad.com

Made in the USA
Monee, IL
01 August 2025